How Not To Say...

Your guide to English pronunciation

by Iciar Senovilla Cearsolo

To my family and friends

ISBN: 978-1543092837

Contents

A personal project and beyond ...

This book is the result of my own desire to speak English more clearly. Just like other Spanish people of my generation I studied English growing up, but this study was focused on written English. In my early twenties I came to the UK to improve my English and complete my studies. Little did I know that I was to meet a charming young man on my very first day. Now, many years later, we are married with two wonderful children.

As for my English, my listening improved very quickly. However, my pronunciation didn't. I tried everything from enrolling on an intensive phonetics course to buying every book on Amazon, but nothing really worked. The breakthrough came when I visited a speech therapist. She told me that some of my Spanish sounds, such as the /s/ sound, were making me sound foreign. This gave me the idea of comparing how English and Spanish sounds were made.

After comparing my accent to a Standard British accent, I extended my research to find out what sounds give international students a foreign accent and so this book was born.

About this book

Why is this book called "How Not To Say"?

When you speak your own language you don't think about the movements of your mouth. They happen automatically. These movements are habits, and may interfere with the way you speak English.

This book will help you identify speech habits that give you a foreign accent. It will also help you replace these habits with English ones.

Who is this book for?

This book is for learners of English all around the world who want to speak English clearly.

You will find this book useful regardless of your level of English, from beginner to advanced.

Who isn't this book for?

This book is NOT for young children. Young children have the ability to learn new sounds by imitation because their speech habits are not ingrained yet. Just let them watch lots of good quality cartoons in English!

British English

This book focuses on British English, paying special attention to Received Pronunciation (RP) which is often referred to as Standard English.

From a student's perspective

On the one hand, this book omits all the information you don't really need to hear. On the other, it includes information that native speakers may not consider important, but that is important to non-native speakers.

How to use this book

I have written this book in simple English and have divided it into small sections. Each section will only take you a few minutes to read. I recommend that you choose a time of day to work on this book, for example during your lunch break or before going to sleep. You only need 10 minutes a day.

Don't give up!

Having a foreign accent is charming. You don't really need to change all the habits that give you a foreign accent. Start with the ones that give you a strong accent. The more of these habits you change, the better your pronunciation will become.

Have fun!

When I showed early copies of this book to my international friends we had a laugh. I hope you do too. Let's get started ...

1

fan - **v**an

fan - van

Identify what gives you a foreign accent

Here are speech habits that you should avoid. You may have several, one, or none of these unwanted habits. Do all the tests to find out!

Test 1- Say "fan" several times: do you close your lips fully when you say the letter **f** in "**f**an"?

O Yes O Sometimes O No

*If your answer is Yes or Sometimes, your pronunciation of "**f**an" will not be clear. It could even be heard as "**p**an".*

Test 2- Say "van" several times: do you close your lips fully when you say the letter **v** in "**v**an"?

O Yes O Sometimes O No

*If your answer is Yes or Sometimes, your pronunciation of "**v**an" could be heard as "**b**an".*

Test 3- Say "Foxton" several times: do you use only your lips (NOT your upper teeth) when you say the letter **f** in "**F**oxton"?

O Yes O Sometimes O No

*If your answer is Yes or Sometimes, your pronunciation of "**F**oxton" may not be clear. It could even be heard as "**H**oxton".*

Test 4- Say "vest" several times: do you round your lips when you say the letter **v** in "**v**est"?

O Yes **O** Sometimes **O** No

*If your answer is Yes or Sometimes, your pronunciation of "**v**est" could be heard as "**w**est".*

Test 5- Say "leaf, leave": do you mumble or forget to say the last sound in "lea**f**" and/or "lea**ve**"?

O Yes **O** Sometimes **O** No

If your answer is Yes or Sometimes, you need to remember to pronounce the sound at the end of the word clearly.

Test 6- Say "leaf, leave" again: do you make the same sound when you say the letters **f** and **ve** in "lea**f**" and "lea**ve**"?

O Yes **O** Sometimes **O** No

*If your answer is Yes or Sometimes, your pronunciation of "lea**ve**" could be heard as "lea**f**" or vice-versa.*

Test 7- Say "leaf, leave" once more: does it take you exactly the same time to say the vowel sound in "l<u>ea</u>f" as in "l<u>ea</u>ve"?

O Yes **O** Sometimes **O** No

If your answer is Yes or Sometimes, you might need to change this.

Keep reading this chapter if you answered Yes or Sometimes to any of these tests. Otherwise, feel free to skip to the next chapter.

Learn how to make these English sounds

Let's look at how to make the sound of the letter **f** in "**f**an" and the sound of the letter **v** in "**v**an".

Did you know that your upper teeth should touch your lower lip when you say the letter **f** in "**f**an" and the letter **v** in "**v**an"?

*

To learn how to say the letter **f** in "**f**an" follow these steps:

1. Get your mouth in the correct position (your upper teeth should touch your lower lip).
2. Blow air out between your upper teeth and lower lip.

Practise making this sound in "**f**an, **F**oxton, so**f**a, lea**f**". The symbol for this sound is /f/. You will also need to make this sound when you say the letters **ph**, **gh**, **fe**, **ff** in "**ph**one, lau**gh**, sa**fe**, o**ff**".

*

To learn how to say the letter **v** in "**v**an" follow these steps:

1. Get your mouth in the correct position (your upper teeth should touch your lower lip).
2. While blowing air out between your upper teeth and lower lip, make a sound with your throat. You should feel a vibration in your throat (put your hand on your throat to feel this vibration). You should also feel a vibration on your lower lip.
3. This is a very short sound: make it as short as possible!

Practise making this sound in "**v**an, **v**est, dri**v**er, in**v**ite". The symbol for this sound is /v/. You will also need to make this sound when you say the letters **ve**, **vv**, **f** in "lea**ve**, sa**vv**y, o**f**". Yes, you need to make the /v/ sound when you say the letter **f** in "o**f**"!

Can you make these sounds at the end of a word?

To learn how to make these sounds at the end of a word as in "lea**f** - lea**ve**", it is important to look at the preceding vowel sounds. Let's see why!

The words "leaf" and "leave" are pronounced with the same vowel sound. However, if you listen to an English person saying these words you may notice that this vowel sound is a little bit shorter in "leaf" than in "leave".

*

To help you say "lea**f**":

1. Make the vowel sound in "leaf" a little shorter than its usual length. In other words, make the vowel sound in "leaf" a little shorter than in "leave".
2. You should feel air coming out of your mouth during the /f/ sound: "lea**f**".

*

To help you say "lea**ve**":

1. Make the vowel sound in "leave" a little longer than its usual length.
2. Please note that your throat always vibrates for English vowels (put your hand on your throat to feel this vibration). Keep this vibration going onto the /v/ sound: "lea**ve**".
3. Make the /v/ sound as short as possible.

Watch and repeat

Go to www.HowNotToSay.com/book to watch a video that will help you with these sounds.

2

thanks - **th**ey

thanks - **th**ey

Identify what gives you a foreign accent

Here are speech habits that you should avoid. You may have several, one, or none of these unwanted habits. Do all the tests to find out!

Test 8- Say "thanks" several times: does your pronunciation of "**th**anks" sound like "**t**anks"?

O Yes **O** Sometimes **O** No

If your answer is Yes or Sometimes, this will give you a strong foreign accent.

Test 9- Say "they" several times: does your pronunciation of "**th**ey" sound like "**d**ay"?

O Yes **O** Sometimes **O** No

If your answer is Yes or Sometimes, you should avoid this.

Test 10- Say "thanks" again: do your upper teeth touch your lower lip when you say the letters **th** in "**th**anks"?

O Yes **O** Sometimes **O** No

*If your answer is Yes or Sometimes, your pronunciation of "**th**anks" could be heard as "**f**anks". Although some native speakers do this, you should avoid it.*

Test 11- Say "than" several times: do your upper teeth touch your lower lip when you say the letters **th** in "**th**an"?

O Yes **O** Sometimes **O** No

*If your answer is Yes or Sometimes, your pronunciation of "***th***an" could be heard as "***v***an". Although some native speakers also do this, you should avoid it.*

Test 12- Say "think" several times: does your pronunciation of "**th**ink" sound similar to "**s**ink"?

O Yes **O** Sometimes **O** No

If your answer is Yes or Sometimes, you should avoid this.

Test 13- Say "tooth, smooth": do you mumble or forget to say the last sound in "too**th**" and/or "smoo**th**"?

O Yes **O** Sometimes **O** No

If your answer is Yes or Sometimes, you need to remember to pronounce the sound at the end of the word clearly.

Test 14- Say "tooth, smooth" again: do you make the same sound when you say the letters **th** in "too**th**, smoo**th**"?

O Yes **O** Sometimes **O** No

If your answer is Yes or Sometimes, you need to be careful with the spelling. The letters ***th*** *in "too****th****" are pronounced as in "****th****anks", and the letters* ***th*** *in "smoo****th****" are pronounced as in "****th****ey".*

Test 15- Say "tooth, smooth" once more: does it take you exactly the same time to say the vowel sound in "tooth" as in "smooth"?

O Yes **O** Sometimes **O** No

If your answer is Yes or Sometimes, you might need to change this.

Keep reading this chapter if you answered Yes or Sometimes to any of these tests. Otherwise, feel free to skip to the next chapter.

Learn how to make these English sounds

Did you know that your mouth needs to be in the same position when you say the letters **th** in "**th**anks" and the letters **th** in "**th**ey"?

Get your mouth in the correct position by placing the tip of your tongue between your upper teeth and your lower teeth. Once your mouth is in this position, what follows depends on whether you are making the sound of the letters **th** in "**th**anks" or the sound of the letters **th** in "**th**ey".

*

To learn how to say the letters **th** in "**th**anks" follow these steps:

1. Put the tip of your tongue between your upper teeth and your lower teeth.
2. Blow air out between your tongue and your teeth.

Practise making this sound in "**th**anks, **th**ink, mara**th**on, too**th**". The symbol for this sound is /θ/.

*

To learn how to say the letters **th** in "**th**ey" follow these steps:

1. Put the tip of your tongue between your upper teeth and your lower teeth.
2. While blowing air out between your tongue and your teeth, make a sound with your throat. You should feel a vibration in your throat (put your hand on your throat to feel this vibration). You should also feel a vibration on your tongue.
3. This is a very short sound: make it as short as possible!

Practise making this sound in "**th**ey, **th**an, fa**th**er, smoo**th**". You will also need to make this sound when you say the letters **the** in "tee**the**". The symbol for this sound is /ð/.

Can you make these sounds at the end of a word?

To learn how to make these sounds at the end of a word as in "too**th** - smoo**th**", it is important to look at the preceding vowel sounds.

The words "tooth" and "smooth" are pronounced with the same vowel sound. However, if you listen to an English person saying these words you may notice that this vowel sound is a little bit shorter in "t<u>oo</u>th" than in "sm<u>oo</u>th".

*

To help you say "too**th**":

1. Make the vowel sound in "t<u>oo</u>th" a little shorter than its usual length. In other words, make the vowel sound in "t<u>oo</u>th" a little shorter than in "sm<u>oo</u>th".
2. You should feel air coming out of your mouth during the /θ/ sound: "too**th**".

*

To help you say "smoo**th**":

1. Make the vowel sound in "sm<u>oo</u>th" a little longer than its usual length.
2. Your throat always vibrates for English vowels (put your hand on your throat to feel this vibration). Keep this vibration going onto the /ð/ sound: "smoo**th**".
3. Make this last sound as short as possible.

Watch and repeat

Go to www.HowNotToSay.com/book to watch a video that will help you with these sounds.

3

sip - **z**ip

sip - **z**ip

Identify what gives you a foreign accent

Here are speech habits that you should avoid. You may have several, one, or none of these unwanted habits. Do all the tests to find out!

Test 16- Say "sip, zip" several times: do you make the same sound when you say the letter **s** in "**s**ip" and the letter **z** in "**z**ip"?

O Yes O Sometimes O No

*If your answer is Yes or Sometimes, your pronunciation of "**z**ip" could be heard as "**s**ip" or vice-versa.*

Test 17- Say "same" several times: do you round your lips when you say the letter **s** in "**s**ame"?

O Yes O Sometimes O No

*If your answer is Yes or Sometimes, your pronunciation of "**s**ame" may not be clear. It could even be heard as "**sh**ame".*

Test 18- Say "sell" several times: do you point the tip of your tongue towards the top of your mouth when you say the letter **s** in "**s**ell"?

O Yes O Sometimes O No

If your answer is Yes or Sometimes, you should avoid this.

Test 19- Say "sink" several times: does your pronunciation of "**s**ink" sound like "**th**ink"?

O Yes **O** Sometimes **O** No

If your answer is Yes or Sometimes, you need to avoid this.

Test 20- Say "Spain" several times: do you say "**es**pain" or "**is**pain" instead of "**S**pain"?

O Yes **O** Sometimes **O** No

If your answer is Yes or Sometimes, your pronunciation of "Spain" will give you a strong foreign accent.

Test 21- Say "sport" several times: do you add a vowel sound between the letters **s** and **p** in "**sp**ort"?

O Yes **O** Sometimes **O** No

*If your answer is Yes or Sometimes, your pronunciation of "**sp**ort" will not be clear. It could even be heard as "**supp**ort".*

Test 22- Say "zoo" and "thanks": do you make the same sound at the start of the words "**z**oo" and "**th**anks"?

O Yes **O** Sometimes **O** No

If your answer is Yes or Sometimes, it will give you a foreign accent.

Test 23- Say "wizard" several times: does your pronunciation of the letter **z** in "wi**z**ard" sounds like **ts** (wi**ts**ard)?

O Yes **O** Sometimes **O** No

If your answer is Yes or Sometimes, you should avoid this.

Test 24- Say "zone" several times: do you press your tongue firmly behind your teeth or against the top of your mouth when you start saying "**z**one"?

O Yes **O** Sometimes **O** No

If your answer is Yes or Sometimes, your pronunciation of "zone" will not be clear. It could even be heard as "Joan".

Test 25- Say "Peter eats biscuits" several times: do you mumble or forget to say the letter **s** in "eat**s**, biscuit**s**"?

O Yes O Sometimes O No

If your answer is Yes or Sometimes, you need to remember to clearly pronounce the letter **s** *at the end of the word/syllable.*

Test 26- Say "price, prize" several times: do you make the same sound when you say the letters **ce** and **ze** in "pri**ce**" and "pri**ze**"?

O Yes O Sometimes O No

*If your answer is Yes or Sometimes, your pronunciation of "pri**ze**" could be heard as "pri**ce**" or vice-versa.*

Test 27- Say "price, prize" again: does it take you exactly the same time to say the vowel sound in "pri̱ce" as in "pri̱ze"?

O Yes O Sometimes O No

If your answer is Yes or Sometimes, you might need to change this.

Keep reading this chapter if you answered Yes or Sometimes to any of these tests. Otherwise, feel free to skip to the next chapter.

Learn how to make these English sounds

Did you know that your mouth needs to be in the same position when you say the letter **s** in "**s**ip" and the letter **z** in "**z**ip"? Get your mouth in the correct position by following these steps:

1. Put your upper teeth and lower teeth together (or almost touching).
2. Smile.
3. Put the tip of your tongue just behind your teeth (either your upper or your lower teeth). If you put your tongue behind your upper teeth, make sure the tip of your

tongue is just behind, but NOT touching, your upper teeth.

Native speakers may round their lips when they say the letter **s** in "**s**ock" and the letter **z** in "**z**oo". This helps them get ready for the vowel sound (**s**ock, **z**oo). I recommend that you start with a smile and then round your lips. However, if you want to round your lips in anticipation of the vowel sound, you will need to be careful NOT to pull your tongue backwards. If you pull your tongue backwards, your pronunciation of "**s**ock" could be heard as "**sh**ock" and your pronunciation of "**z**oo" might not be clear.

*

To learn how to say the letter **s** in "**s**ip" follow these steps:

1. Get your mouth in the correct position, as described above. That is, put your upper and lower teeth together (or almost touching), smile and put the tip of your tongue just behind your teeth.
2. Blow air out of your mouth. Since your teeth are together (or almost touching) you will hear air hitting your teeth on its way out of your mouth.

Practise making this sound in "**s**ip, **s**ame, **s**ell, **s**ink, **S**pain, **s**port, eat**s**, bi**s**cuit**s**, in**s**ect, bu**s**, **s**ock". The symbol for this sound is /s/. You will also need to make this sound when you say the letters **ss**, **c**, **ce**, **se**, **sc**, **st**, **s** in "dre**ss**, **c**ity, pri**ce**, hor**se**, **sc**ien**ce**, li**st**en, cat**s**".

If you find it difficult to make the /s/ sound in "**S**pain, **s**port" follow these steps:

1. Put your upper and lower teeth together BEFORE you start making the /s/ sound.

2. Start making the /s/ sound.
3. Keep making this sound UNTIL your lips are fully closed for /p/ (**Sp**ain, **sp**ort). In other words, keep making the /s/ sound until your mouth is in position for the next sound.
4. As Lucie, a native English teacher from Nottingham, advised me: concentrate on the /s/ sound and the vowel sound: **S**p**ai**n, **s**p**o**rt. As for the sound in-between, make it as quickly as possible.

*

To learn how to say the letter **z** in "**z**ip" follow these steps:

1. Put your mouth in the same position as if you were going to say the letter **s** in "**s**ip". That is, put your upper and lower teeth together (or almost touching), smile and put the tip of your tongue just behind your teeth.
2. While blowing air out of your mouth, make a sound with your throat. You should feel a vibration in your throat (put your hand on your throat to feel this vibration).
3. This is a very short sound: make it as short as possible!

Practise making this sound in "**z**ip, **z**oo, **z**one, wi**z**ard, la**z**y". The symbol for this sound is /z/. You will also need to make this sound when you say the letters **zz**, **ze**, **se**, **ss**, **s** in "bu**zz**, pri**ze**, plea**se**, sci**ss**ors, mu**s**ic". Yes, the letters **se** in "plea**se**", the letters **ss** in "sci**ss**ors", the last letter **s** in "scissor**s**" and the middle **s** in "mu**s**ic" are pronounced with the /z/ sound.

Can you make these sounds at the end of a word?

To learn how to make these sounds at the end of a word as in "pri**ce** - pri**ze**", it is important to look at the preceding vowel sounds.

The words "price" and "prize" are pronounced with the same vowel sound. However, if you listen to an English person saying these words you may notice that this vowel sound is a little bit shorter in "price" than in "prize".

*

To help you say "pri**ce**":

1. Make the vowel sound in "price" a little shorter than its usual length. In other words, make the vowel sound in "price" a little shorter than in "prize".
2. You should feel air hitting your teeth during the /s/ sound: "pri**ce**".

*

To help you say "pri**ze**":

1. Make the vowel sound in "prize" a little longer than its usual length.
2. Your throat always vibrates for English vowels (put your hand on your throat to feel this vibration). Keep this vibration going onto the /z/ sound: "pri**ze**".
3. Make the /z/ sound as short as possible.

Watch and repeat

Go to www.HowNotToSay.com/book to watch a video that will help you with these sounds.

4

ship - tele**vi**sion

ship - televi**si**on

Identify what gives you a foreign accent

Here are speech habits that you should avoid. You may have several, one, or none of these unwanted habits. Do all the tests to find out!

Test 28- Say "ship, English, television" several times: do you pronounce these words with the /s/ sound?

O Yes O Sometimes O No

*If your answer is Yes or Sometimes, your pronunciation of "**sh**ip" will be heard as "**s**ip". As for your pronunciation of "Engli**sh**" and "televi**si**on", it will sound foreign.*

Test 29- Say "shopping" several times: do you press your tongue firmly behind your teeth or against the top of your mouth when you start saying "**sh**opping"?

O Yes O Sometimes O No

*If your answer is Yes or Sometimes, your pronunciation of "**sh**opping" could be heard as "**ch**opping".*

Keep reading this chapter if you answered Yes or Sometimes to any of these tests. Otherwise, feel free to skip to the next chapter.

Learn how to make these English sounds

Did you know that you DO NOT have to make the /s/ sound in the words "ship" and "television"?

Let's look at how to say the letters **sh** in "**sh**ip" and the letters **si** in "televi**si**on". Get your mouth in the correct position by following these steps:

1. Put your upper teeth and lower teeth together (or almost touching).
2. Round your lips a little.
3. Pull your tongue backwards but do not pull it back too much.

Once your mouth is in this position, what follows depends on whether you are making the sound of the letters **sh** in "**sh**ip" or the sound of the letters **si** in "televi**si**on".

*

To learn how to say the letters **sh** in "**sh**ip" follow these steps:

1. Get your mouth in the correct position: put your upper and lower teeth together (or almost touching), round your lips and pull your tongue backwards.
2. Blow air out of your mouth. Since your teeth are together (or almost touching), you will hear air hitting your teeth on its way out of your mouth.

Practise making this sound in "**sh**ip, **sh**ampoo, **sh**e, **sh**opping, pu**sh**, Engli**sh**". The symbol for this sound is /ʃ/. You will also need to make this sound when you say the letters **ch** in "**ch**ef, **ch**alet, **ch**auffeur", the letters **ti** in "na**ti**on, po**ti**on, lo**ti**on", the letters **ci** in "magi**ci**an, deli**ci**ous, musi**ci**an", the letters **ssi** in "mi**ssi**on, discu**ssi**on, confe**ssi**on", the letters **ce** in "o**ce**an" and the letter **s** in "**s**ugar".

*

To learn how to say the letters **si** in "televi**si**on" follow these steps:

1. Put your mouth in the same position as if you were going to say "**sh**ip". That is, put your upper and lower teeth together (or almost touching), round your lips and pull your tongue backwards.
2. While blowing air out of your mouth, make a sound with your throat. You should feel a vibration in your throat (put your hand on your throat to feel this vibration).
3. This is a very short sound: make it as short as possible!

Practise making this sound in "televi**si**on, explo**si**on, divi**si**on". The symbol for this sound is /ʒ/. You will also need to make this sound when you say the letters **ge** in "bei**ge**", the letters **ges** in "Bru**ges**", the letters **su** in "trea**su**re, mea**su**re, lei**su**re" and the letter **s** in "u**s**ual".

The /ʒ/ sound is not very common in English. It ONLY appears in a few English words and never at the start of a word.

Can you make these sounds at the end of a word?

Let's look at how to make these sounds at the end of a word as in "Engli**sh** - bei**ge**".

*

To help you say "Engli**sh**":

1. Make sure you say "Engli**sh**" (NOT "Englis"). You need to round your lips and pull your tongue backwards at the end of the word "Engli**sh**".
2. Make sure you hear air hitting your teeth while you make the /ʃ/ sound: "Engli**sh**".

*

To help you say "bei**ge**":

1. Make the vowel sound in "b<u>e</u>ige" a little longer than its usual length.
2. Your throat always vibrates for English vowels (put your hand on your throat to feel this vibration). Keep this vibration going onto the /ʒ/ sound: "bei**ge**".
3. Make this last sound as short as possible.

Watch and repeat

Go to www.HowNotToSay.com/book to watch a video that will help you with these sounds.

5

pea - **b**ee

pea - bee

Identify what gives you a foreign accent

Here are speech habits that you should avoid. You may have several, one, or none of these unwanted habits. Do all the tests to find out!

Test 30- Put a thin piece of paper in front of your mouth and say "pea": does the paper stay still (not move)?

O Yes O Sometimes O No

*If your answer is Yes or Sometimes, your pronunciation of "**p**ea" may not be clear. It may even be heard as "**b**ee".*

Test 31- Say "rebel" several times: do you close your mouth gently (instead of firmly) when you say the letter **b** in "re**b**el"?

O Yes O Sometimes O No

*If your answer is Yes or Sometimes, your pronunciation of "re**b**el" will be half way between "re**b**el" and "re**v**el".*

Test 32- Say "lap, lab" several times: does your pronunciation of "la**b**" sound like "la**p**" or vice-versa?

O Yes O Sometimes O No

If your answer is Yes or Sometimes, you need to work on these sounds.

Test 33- Say "lap, lab" again: does it take you exactly the same time to say the vowel sound in "lap" as in "lab"?

O Yes **O** Sometimes **O** No

If your answer is Yes or Sometimes, you might need to change this.

Keep reading this chapter if you answered Yes or Sometimes to any of these tests. Otherwise, feel free to skip to the next chapter.

Learn how to make these English sounds

Your mouth needs to be fully closed when you start saying "**p**ea" and "**b**ee".

*

To learn how to say the letter **p** in "**p**ea" follow these steps:

1. Close your mouth fully.
2. Try to blow air out of your mouth. The air will stay inside your mouth because your mouth is fully closed!
3. Open your mouth. As you open your mouth, the air will suddenly escape.

Practise making this sound in "**p**ea, o**p**en, ketchu**p**". The symbol for this sound is /p/. You will also need to make this sound when you say the letters **pp** in "ha**pp**y, su**pp**ose, a**pp**ear" and the letters **pe** in "ty**pe**, envelo**pe**, telesco**pe**".

Many native speakers blow out a lot of air when they make this sound at the start of a stressed syllable as in "**pea**, su**ppose**, a**ppear**". If one of these speakers had a thin paper in front of their mouth, the paper would move. Be careful NOT to get carried away! As my nine year old daughter advises me, the important thing is to make a sharp /p/ sound.

*

To learn how to say the letter **b** in "**b**ee" follow these steps:

1. Close your mouth fully.
2. Try to blow air out of your mouth. The air will stay inside your mouth because your mouth is fully closed!
3. Make a sound with your throat while you open your mouth. As you open your mouth, you will notice a vibration in your throat.

Practise making this sound in "**b**ee, re**b**el, we**b**". The symbol for this sound is /b/. You will also need to make this sound when you say the letters **be** in "descri**be**, tu**be**, glo**be**", the letters **bb** in "ra**bb**it" and the letters **bu** in "**bu**ild".

Can you make these sounds at the end of a word?

I have always found it difficult to make the last sound in words such as "la**p** - la**b**", "ba**ck** - ba**g**" and "be**t** - be**d**". So much so that I had to call a speech therapist to help me with these sounds.

Let's look at "la**p** - la**b**". These words are pronounced with the same vowel sound. However, if you listen to an English person saying these words you may notice that this vowel sound is a little bit shorter in "lap" than in "lab".

*

To help you say "la**p**":

1. Make the vowel sound in "lap" a little shorter than its usual length. In other words, make the vowel sound in "lap" a little shorter than in "lab".
2. Make sure you feel air coming out of your mouth at the end of the word "la**p**".

*

To help you say "la**b**":

1. Make the vowel sound in "l<u>a</u>b" a little longer than its usual length.
2. Your throat always vibrates for English vowels (put your hand on your throat to feel this vibration). Keep this vibration going onto the /b/ sound: "la**b**".

If you still have problems saying "la**b**":

1. Check that your mouth is fully closed when you start saying /b/.
2. Make sure you can feel, and also hear, the vibration in your throat when you say /b/.

Do you still find it difficult to say "la**b**"? There is something else you can do. As the speech therapist recommended to me, try adding a little vowel at the end of the word. This will help you keep the vibration in your throat. Do this until you get used to keeping the vibration in your throat.

Watch and repeat

Go to www.HowNotToSay.com/book to watch a video that will help you with these sounds.

6

cold - **g**old

cold - **g**old

Identify what gives you a foreign accent

Here are speech habits that you should avoid. You may have several, one, or none of these unwanted habits. Do all the tests to find out!

Test 34- Put a thin piece of paper in front of your mouth and say "cold": does the paper stay still (not move)?

O Yes O Sometimes O No

*If your answer is Yes or Sometimes, your pronunciation of "***c***old" may not be clear. It may even be heard as "***g***old".*

Test 35- Say "yoga" several times: does the back of your tongue get close to (but NOT firmly touch) the top of your mouth when you say the letter **g** in "yoga"?

O Yes O Sometimes O No

*If your answer is Yes or Sometimes, your pronunciation of "yo***g***a" may not be clear.*

Test 36- Say "next" several times: does your pronunciation of "ne**x**t" sound like "ne**s**t"?

O Yes O Sometimes O No

If your answer is Yes or Sometimes, you should avoid this.

Test 37- Say "pig, magnetic" several times: do you make a sound that is harsh (unpleasant to the ear) when you say the letter **g** in "pi**g**" and/or "ma**g**netic"?

O Yes O Sometimes O No

If your answer is Yes or Sometimes, this will give you a strong foreign accent.

Test 38- Say "back, bag" several times: does your pronunciation of "ba**g**" sound like "ba**ck**" or vice-versa?

O Yes O Sometimes O No

If your answer is Yes or Sometimes, you need to work on these sounds.

Test 39- Say "back, bag" again: does it take you exactly the same time to say the vowel sound in "b<u>a</u>ck" as in "b<u>a</u>g"?

O Yes O Sometimes O No

If your answer is Yes or Sometimes, you might need to change this.

Keep reading this chapter if you answered Yes or Sometimes to any of these tests. Otherwise, feel free to skip to the next chapter.

Learn how to make these English sounds

The back of your tongue should firmly touch the top of your mouth when you start saying "**c**old" and "**g**old".

*

To learn how to say the letter **c** in "**c**old" follow these steps:

1. Press the back of your tongue firmly against the top of your mouth.
2. Try to blow air out of your mouth. The air will not come out because your tongue is blocking the exit.

3. Now, drop your tongue down. As you drop your tongue down, the air will suddenly escape.

Practise making this sound in "**c**old, ba**c**on, mimi**c**". The symbol for this sound is /k/. You will also need to make this sound when you say the letters **k**, **ke**, **ck**, **cc**, **ch**, **che**, **qu**, **que** in "**k**ilo, ma**ke**, so**ck**, a**cc**ount, s**ch**ool, heada**che**, **qu**iche, **que**ue". Please note that the letter **x** in "ne**x**t, si**x**ty, bo**x**es" is pronounced with a /k/ sound followed by a /s/ sound.

Many native speakers blow out a lot of air when they make this sound at the start of a stressed syllable as in "**cold**, **ki**lo, a**ccount**, **quiche**, **queue**". If one of these speakers had a thin piece of paper in front of their mouth, the paper would move.

*

To learn how to say the letter **g** in "**g**old" follow these steps:

1. Press the back of your tongue firmly against the top of your mouth.
2. Try to blow air out of your mouth. The air will not come out because your tongue is blocking the exit.
3. Make a sound with your throat while you drop your tongue down. As you drop your tongue down, you will notice a vibration in your throat.

Practise making this sound in "**g**old, yo**g**a, ma**g**netic, pi**g**". The symbol for this sound is /g/. You will also need to make this sound when you say the letters **gu** in "**gu**ess, **gu**itar, **gu**ide" and the letters **gue**, **gh**, **gg** in "catalo**gue**, **gh**ost, e**gg**".

Can you make these sounds at the end of a word?

To learn how to make these sounds at the end of a word as in "ba**ck** - ba**g**", you should look at the preceding vowel sounds.

If you listen to an English person saying "ba**ck** - ba**g**" you may notice that the same vowel sound is a little bit shorter in "back" than in "bag".

*

To help you say "ba**ck**":

1. Make the vowel sound in "back" a little shorter than in the word "bag".
2. Make sure you feel air coming out of your mouth at the end of the word "ba**ck**".

*

To help you say "ba**g**":

1. Make the vowel sound in "bag" a little longer than in the word "back".
2. Your throat always vibrates for English vowels (put your hand on your throat to feel this vibration). Keep this vibration going onto the /g/ sound: "ba**g**".

If you still have problems saying "ba**g**":

1. Check that the back of your tongue firmly touches the top of your mouth when you start saying /g/.
2. Make sure you can feel, and also hear, the vibration in your throat when you say /g/.

If you still find it difficult to say "ba**g**", try adding a little vowel at the end of the word. This will help you keep the vibration in your throat. Do this until you get used to keeping the vibration in your throat.

Watch and repeat

Go to www.HowNotToSay.com/book to watch a video that will help you with these sounds.

7

town - **d**own

town - **d**own

Identify what gives you a foreign accent

Here are speech habits that you should avoid. You may have several, one, or none of these unwanted habits. Do all the tests to find out!

Test 40- Put a thin piece of paper in front of your mouth and say "town": does the paper stay still (not move)?

O Yes O Sometimes O No

*If your answer is Yes or Sometimes, your pronunciation of "**t**own" may not be clear. It may even be heard as "**d**own".*

Test 41- Say "town, down" several times: does the tip of your tongue touch your teeth when you say the letter **t** in "**t**own" and/or the letter **d** in "**d**own"?

O Yes O Sometimes O No

If your answer is Yes or Sometimes, you should avoid this.

Test 42- Say "tip, dip" several times: do you point the tip of your tongue towards the top of your mouth when you say the letter **t** in "**t**ip" and/or the letter **d** in "**d**ip"?

O Yes O Sometimes O No

If your answer is Yes or Sometimes, you should avoid this.

Test 43- Say "today" several times: do you put the tip of your tongue between your upper and lower teeth when you say the letter **d** in "to**d**ay"?

O Yes **O** Sometimes **O** No

*If your answer is Yes or Sometimes, you will actually be saying "to**they**" instead of "to**day**".*

Test 44- Say "bet, bed" several times: does your pronunciation of "be**d**" sound like "be**t**" or vice-versa?

O Yes **O** Sometimes **O** No

If your answer is Yes or Sometimes, you need to work on these sounds when they appear at the end of a word.

Test 45- Say "bet, bed" again: does it take you exactly the same time to say the vowel sound in "b<u>e</u>t" as in "b<u>e</u>d"?

O Yes **O** Sometimes **O** No

If your answer is Yes or Sometimes, you might need to change this.

Keep reading this chapter if you answered Yes or Sometimes to any of these tests. Otherwise, feel free to skip to the next chapter.

Learn how to make these English sounds

Let's look at how to say the letter **t** in "**t**own" and the letter **d** in "**d**own". First, get your mouth in the correct position by following these steps:

1. Put the tip of your tongue just behind your upper teeth, making sure the tip of your tongue is just behind (but does NOT touch) your upper teeth.
2. With the tip of your tongue just behind your upper teeth, press your tongue firmly against the top of your mouth.

Once your mouth is in this position, what follows depends on whether you are making the sound of the letter **t** in "**t**own" or the sound of the letter **d** in "**d**own".

*

To learn how to say the letter **t** in "**t**own" follow these steps:

1. Get your mouth in the correct position: put the tip of your tongue just behind your upper teeth and press your tongue firmly against the top of your mouth.
2. Try to blow air out of your mouth. The air will stay inside your mouth because your tongue is blocking the exit.
3. Now, drop your tongue down. As you drop your tongue down, the air will suddenly escape.

Practise making this sound in "**t**own, **t**ip, ho**t**el, ca**t**". The symbol for this sound is /t/. You will also need to make this sound when you say the letters **tt**, **th**, **te**, **ght** in "a**tt**ack, **Th**ailand, no**te**, ei**ght**" and the letters **ed** in "stopp**ed**, look**ed**, kiss**ed**". Yes, the letters **ed** in "stopp**ed**, look**ed**, kiss**ed**" are pronounced with one sound, the /t/ sound.

Many native speakers blow out a lot of air when they make this sound at the start of a stressed syllable as in "**town**, **tip**, ho**tel**, a**ttack**, **Thai**land". If one of these speakers had a thin piece of paper in front of their mouth, the paper would move.

It is interesting to note that some native speakers may stop this sound in the throat when they say the letter **t** in words such as "don'**t**, tha**t**, bu**t**, no**t**, pu**t**, ca**t**". Don't worry! You don't have to do this. Just be aware of it.

It is also interesting to note that most native speakers of American English make a sound similar to /d/ when they say words such as "Sea**tt**le, Na**t**alie, wri**t**er".

*

To learn how to say the letter **d** in "**d**own" follow these steps:

1. Get your mouth in the correct position: put the tip of your tongue just behind your upper teeth and press your tongue firmly against the top of your mouth.
2. Try to blow air out of your mouth. The air will stay inside your mouth because your tongue is blocking the exit.
3. Make a sound with your throat while you drop your tongue down. As you drop your tongue down, you will notice a vibration in your throat.

Practise making this sound when you say the letter **d** in "**d**own, **d**ip, to**d**ay, sa**d**, starte**d**, affor**ded**". The symbol for this sound is /d/. You will also need to make this sound when you say the letters **ed** in "open**ed**, play**ed**, boil**ed**" and the letters **dd** in "la**dd**er". Yes, the letters **ed** in "open**ed**, play**ed**, boil**ed**" are pronounced with one sound, the /d/ sound.

Can you make these sounds at the end of a word?

To learn how to make these sounds at the end of a word as in "be**t** - be**d**", you should look at the preceding vowel sounds.

The words "bet" and "bed" are pronounced with the same vowel sound. However, if you listen to an English person saying these words you may notice that this vowel sound is a little bit shorter in "bet" than in "bed".

*

To help you say "be**t**":

1. Make the vowel sound in "bet" a little shorter than in the word "bed".

town - down

2. Make sure you feel air coming out of your mouth at the end of the word "be**t**".

*

To help you say "be**d**":

1. Make the vowel sound in "bed" a little longer than in the word "bet".
2. Your throat always vibrates for English vowels (put your hand on your throat to feel this vibration). Keep this vibration going onto the /d/ sound: "be**d**".

If you still have problems saying "be**d**":

1. Check that your tongue firmly touches the top of your mouth when you start making the last sound in "be**d**".
2. Make sure you can feel, and also hear, the vibration in your throat when you say /d/.

If you still find it difficult to say "be**d**", try adding a little vowel at the end of the word. This will help you keep the vibration in your throat. Do this until you get used to keeping the vibration in your throat.

Watch and repeat

Go to www.HowNotToSay.com/book to watch a video that will help you with these sounds.

8

chain - **J**ane

chain - **J**ane

Identify what gives you a foreign accent

Here are speech habits that you should avoid. You may have several, one, or none of these unwanted habits. Do all the tests to find out!

Test 46- Say "chain - Jane" several times: does the tip of your tongue touch your teeth or get very close to your teeth when you say the letters **ch** in "**ch**ain" and/or the letter **j** in "**J**ane"?

O Yes   O Sometimes   O No

If your answer is Yes or Sometimes, you should avoid this.

Test 47- Say "chip" several times: does your pronunciation of "**ch**ip" sound like "**sh**ip" or "**s**ip"?

O Yes   O Sometimes   O No

*If your answer is Yes or Sometimes, your pronunciation of "**ch**ip" will not be clear.*

Test 48- Say "choose" several times: does your pronunciation of the letters **ch** in "**ch**oose" sound like **ti** (tioose)?

O Yes   O Sometimes   O No

*If your answer is Yes or Sometimes, your pronunciation of "**ch**oose" will not be clear.*

Test 49- Say "jet" several times: does your pronunciation of "**j**et" sound like "**y**et"?

O Yes **O** Sometimes **O** No

If your answer is Yes or Sometimes, your pronunciation of "jet" will not be clear.

Test 50- Say "John" several times: does your tongue touch (but NOT press) the top of your mouth when you say the letter **j** in "**J**ohn"?

O Yes **O** Sometimes **O** No

If your answer is Yes or Sometimes, your pronunciation of "John" may not be clear.

Test 51- Say "chain, Jane": are your lips relaxed when you say the letters **ch** in "**ch**ain" and/or the letter **j** in "**J**ane"?

O Yes **O** Sometimes **O** No

If your answer is Yes or Sometimes, you need to learn how to pronounce these English sounds correctly.

Test 52- Say "rich, bridge" several times: is the last sound you make in "bri**dge**" identical to the last sound you make in "ri**ch**"?

O Yes **O** Sometimes **O** No

If your answer is Yes or Sometimes, you should avoid this.

Test 53- Say "rich, bridge" again: does it take you exactly the same time to say the vowel sound in "rich" as in "bridge"?

O Yes **O** Sometimes **O** No

If your answer is Yes or Sometimes, you might need to change this.

Keep reading this chapter if you answered Yes or Sometimes to any of these tests. Otherwise, feel free to skip to the next chapter.

Learn how to make these English sounds

Did you know that your mouth needs to be in the same position when you say the letters **ch** in "**ch**ain" and the letter **j** in "Jane"? Get your mouth in the correct position by following these steps:

1. Put your upper teeth and lower teeth together (or almost touching).
2. Round your lips a little.
3. Pull your tongue backwards but do not pull it back too much.
4. Press your tongue firmly against the top of your mouth.

Once your mouth is in this position, what follows depends on whether you are making the sound of the letters **ch** in "**ch**ain" or the sound of the letter **J** in "**J**ane".

*

To learn how to say the letters **ch** in "**ch**ain" follow these steps:

1. Get your mouth in the correct position: put your upper and lower teeth together (or almost touching), round your lips, pull your tongue backwards and press your tongue firmly against the top of your mouth.
2. Try to blow air out of your mouth. The air will stay inside your mouth because your tongue is blocking the exit.
3. Now, drop your tongue down **a little** bit. As you drop your tongue down a little, the air will pass between your tongue and the top of your mouth, hitting your teeth on its way out of your mouth.

Practise making this sound in "**ch**ain, **ch**ip, **ch**oose, tea**ch**er, bea**ch**". The symbol for this sound is /tʃ/. You will also need to make this sound in "wa**tch**, pic**t**ure".

*

To learn how to say the letter **J** in "**J**ane" follow these steps:

1. Put your mouth in the same position as if you were going to say the letters **ch** in "**ch**ain". That is, put your upper and lower teeth together (or almost touching), round your lips, pull your tongue backwards and press your tongue firmly against the top of your mouth.
2. Try to blow air out of your mouth. The air will stay inside your mouth because your tongue is still blocking the exit.
3. Make a sound with your throat while you drop your tongue down a little. You should feel a vibration in your throat (put your hand on your throat to feel this vibration).

Practise making this sound in "**J**ane, **j**et, **J**ohn, pro**j**ect". The symbol for this sound is /dʒ/. You will also need to make this sound when you say the letters **ge**, **dge** in "**Ge**or**ge**, bri**dge**" and the letter **g** in "**g**ym, **g**iant".

Can you make these sounds at the end of a word?

Let's look at how to make these sounds at the end of a word as in "ri**ch**, bri**dge**".

*

To help you say "ri**ch**":

1. First, make sure that your upper and lower teeth are together (or almost touching), your lips are rounded and your tongue is pulled backwards.
2. Second, remember to press your tongue firmly against the top of your mouth.
3. Now drop your tongue down a little. As you drop it down a little, you should hear air hitting your teeth.

*

To help you say "bri**dge**":

1. Make the vowel sound in "bridge" a little longer than its usual length.
2. Your throat always vibrates for English vowels (put your hand on your throat to feel this vibration). Keep this vibration going onto the last sound: "bri**dge**".

If you still have problems saying "bri**dge**":

1. Check that your mouth is in the correct position for this sound.
2. Make sure you can feel, and also hear, the vibration in your throat.

If you still find it difficult to say "bri**dge**", try adding a little vowel at the end of the word. This will help you keep the vibration in your throat. Do this until you get used to keeping the vibration in your throat.

Watch and repeat

Go to www.HowNotToSay.com/book to watch a video that will help you with these sounds.

9

album

album

Identify what gives you a foreign accent

Here are speech habits that you should avoid. You may have several, one, or none of these unwanted habits. Do all the tests to find out!

Test 54- Say "album" several times: do you say "albu**n**" instead of "albu**m**"?

O Yes O Sometimes O No

*If your answer is Yes or Sometimes, your pronunciation of "albu**m**" may not be clear.*

Test 55- Say "room" several times: do you mumble or forget to say the letter **m** in "roo**m**"?

O Yes O Sometimes O No

*If your answer is Yes or Sometimes, you need to remember to pronounce the letter **m** clearly at the end of the word "roo**m**".*

Keep reading this chapter if you answered Yes or Sometimes to any of these tests. Otherwise, feel free to skip to the next chapter.

Learn how to make this English sound

Your lips need to be fully closed WHILE you say the letter **m** in "albu**m**". With the lips fully closed, make a sound with your throat.

Practise making this sound in "albu**m**, roo**m**, to**m**ato, **m**ap". The symbol for this sound is /m/. You will also need to make this sound when you say the letters **mm**, **mb**, **mn**, **me** in "su**mm**er, cli**mb**, colu**mn**, ti**me**".

Try these experiments

Experiment 1- Pinch your nose while you say "albu**m**, roo**m**, to**m**ato, **m**ap, su**mm**er, cli**mb**, colu**mn**, ti**me**". It should give the impression that you have a cold. Why? The air escapes through the nose for this sound.

Experiment 2- Put your hand on your throat when you make the /m/ sound. You should feel your throat vibrate a little when you make this sound. You should also feel a little vibration in your nose and on your lips.

Watch and repeat

Go to www.HowNotToSay.com/book to watch a video that will help you with this sound.

10

net

net

Identify what gives you a foreign accent

Here are speech habits that you should avoid. You may have several, one, or none of these unwanted habits. Do all the tests to find out!

Test 56- Say "net" several times: does your pronunciation of "**n**et" sound like "**l**et"?

O Yes O Sometimes O No

If your answer is Yes or Sometimes, you need to avoid this.

Test 57- Say "thin" several times: do you leave the tip of your tongue behind your lower teeth when you say the letter **n** in "thi**n**"?

O Yes O Sometimes O No

*If your answer is Yes or Sometimes, your pronunciation of "thi**n**" could be heard as "thi**ng**".*

Test 58- Say "sun" several times: do you close your lips when you say the letter **n** in "su**n**"?

O Yes O Sometimes O No

*If your answer is Yes or Sometimes, your pronunciation of "su**n**" could be heard as "su**m**".*

Test 59- Say "Amazon" several times: do you mumble or forget to say the letter **n** in "Amazo**n**"?

O Yes **O** Sometimes **O** No

*If your answer is Yes or Sometimes, you need to remember to pronounce the letter **n** clearly at the end of the word "Amazo**n**".*

Keep reading this chapter if you answered Yes or Sometimes to any of these tests. Otherwise, feel free to skip to the next chapter.

Learn how to make this English sound

Get your mouth in the correct position by following these steps:

1. Put the tip of your tongue just behind your upper teeth, making sure the tip of your tongue is just behind (but does NOT touch) your upper teeth.
2. With the tip of your tongue just behind your upper teeth, press your tongue firmly against the top of your mouth.

Your mouth needs to be in this position WHILE you say the letter **n** in "**n**et". With your mouth in this position, make a sound with your throat.

Practise making this sound in "**n**et, thi**n**, su**n**, Amazo**n**, po**n**y". The symbol for this sound is /n/. You will also need to make this sound when you say the letters **nn**, **kn**, **gn**, **ne** in "di**nn**er, **kn**ow, desi**gn**, pho**ne**".

Please note that the tip of your tongue will need to touch your teeth when you make the /n/ sound in words such as "mo**n**th, te**n**th". This will help you pronounce the letters **th** in these words: "mon**th**, ten**th**".

Try these experiments

Experiment 1- Pinch your nose while you say "**n**et, thi**n**, su**n**, Amazo**n**, po**n**y, di**nn**er, **kn**ow, desi**gn**, pho**ne**". It should give the impression that you have a cold. The air escapes through the nose for this sound.

Experiment 2- Put your hand on your throat when you make the /n/ sound. You should feel your throat vibrate a little when you make this sound. You should also feel a little vibration in your nose.

Watch and repeat

Go to www.HowNotToSay.com/book to watch a video that will help you with this sound.

11

sing

sing

Identify what gives you a foreign accent

Here are speech habits that you should avoid. You may have several, one, or none of these unwanted habits. Do all the tests to find out!

Test 60- Say "sing" several times: does your pronunciation of "si**ng**" sound like "si**nk**"?

O Yes **O** Sometimes **O** No

*If your answer is Yes or Sometimes, your pronunciation of "si**ng**" will give you a strong foreign accent.*

Test 61- Say "sing, English, link" several times: does the tip or front of your tongue touch the top of your mouth when you say the letter **n** in "si**n**g, E**n**glish, li**n**k"?

O Yes **O** Sometimes **O** No

*If your answer is Yes or Sometimes, please note that the letter **n** in "si**n**g, E**n**glish, li**n**k" should NOT be pronounced with the /n/ sound.*

Keep reading this chapter if you answered Yes or Sometimes to any of these tests. Otherwise, feel free to skip to the next chapter.

Learn how to make this English sound

The letters **ng** in "si**ng**" are pronounced with the /ŋ/ sound. To make this sound, press the back of your tongue firmly against the top of your mouth. Your mouth needs to be in this position WHILE you say the letters **ng** in "si**ng**". With your mouth in this position, make a sound with your throat.

You will have to make this sound followed by the /g/ sound in "E**ng**lish, stro**ng**er, stro**ng**est". You will have to make this sound followed by the /k/ sound in "li**nk**, mo**nk**ey, u**nc**le, co**nq**uer".

What happens with "sing, king, eating"?

Most native speakers DO NOT say /g/ in "si**ng**, ki**ng**, eati**ng**". This is how they pronounce the letters **ng** at the end of a word. Practise saying these words with a /ŋ/ sound at the end.

Try these experiments

Experiment 1- Pinch your nose while you say "E**ng**lish, stro**ng**er, stro**ng**est, li**nk**, mo**nk**ey, u**nc**le, co**nq**uer, si**ng**, ki**ng**, eati**ng**". It should give the impression that you have a cold. The air escapes through the nose for this sound.

Experiment 2- Put your hand on your throat when you make this sound. You should feel your throat vibrate a little when you make this sound. You should also feel a little vibration in your nose.

Watch and repeat

Go to www.HowNotToSay.com/book to watch a video that will help you with this sound.

12

last

last

Identify what gives you a foreign accent

Here are speech habits that you should avoid. You may have several, one, or none of these habits. Do all the tests to find out!

Test 62- Say "let" several times: do the sides of your tongue touch the top of your mouth when you say the letter **l** in "**l**et"?

O Yes **O** Sometimes **O** No

*If your answer is Yes or Sometimes, you are probably saying "**n**et" instead of "**l**et".*

Test 63- Say "light, collect" several times: does your pronunciation of "**l**ight, co**ll**ect" sound like "**r**ight, co**rr**ect"?

O Yes **O** Sometimes **O** No

If your answer is Yes or Sometimes, please note that the meaning of the word changes if you say /r/ instead of /l/.

Test 64- Say "hill" several times: do you make a long sound when you say the letters **ll** in "hi**ll**"?

O Yes **O** Sometimes **O** No

If your answer is Yes or Sometimes, you should avoid this.

Test 65- Say "last, milk" several times: do you make the same sound when you say the letter **l** in "last" and in "milk"?

O Yes **O** Sometimes **O** No

It is okay if your answer is Yes or Sometimes. However, it is important to note that many English people make a different /l/ sound in "last" and "milk".

Keep reading this chapter if you answered Yes or Sometimes to any of these tests. Otherwise, feel free to skip to the next chapter.

Learn how to make this English sound

Let's look at how to say the letter **l** in "last". First, get your mouth in the correct position by following these steps:

1. Put the tip of your tongue just behind your upper teeth, making sure the tip of your tongue is just behind (but does NOT touch) your upper teeth.
2. With the tip of your tongue just behind your upper teeth, press the very front part of your tongue against the top of your mouth.

Your mouth needs to be in this position WHILE you say the letter **l** in "last". With your mouth in this position, make a sound with your throat.

Practise making this sound in "last, let, light". The symbol for this sound is /l/. You also need to make this sound when you say the letters **ll** in "collect, yellow, pillow".

If you find it very difficult to make this sound, you could try making this sound with the tip of your tongue between your upper teeth and lower teeth. Once you are able to make this sound, try making it as described above.

last

What happens with "milk, hill"?

Many English people make a different /l/ sound in words such as "milk, hill". If you want to learn how to make this second type of /l/ sound you can follow these steps:

1. Press the very front of your tongue against the top of your mouth as for the **l** in "**l**ast".
2. As David, a native voice teacher, advised me: imagine you have a heavy ball on your tongue pressing your tongue down. Due to the 'imaginary heavy ball' the tip of your tongue will be more upright than for the letter **l** in "**l**ast".
3. With your tongue in this position, make a short sound with your throat.

Watch and repeat

Go to www.HowNotToSay.com/book to watch a video that will help you with this sound.

13

red

red

Identify what gives you a foreign accent

Here are speech habits that you should avoid. You may have several, one, or none of these habits. Do all the tests to find out!

Test 66- Say "red" several times: does your tongue touch or get very close to the top of your mouth when you say the letter **r** in "**r**ed"?

O Yes O Sometimes O No

If your answer is Yes or Sometimes, it will give you a foreign accent.

Test 67- Say "red" again: does your tongue get very close to, or even touch, the back of your mouth when you say the letter **r** in "**r**ed"?

O Yes O Sometimes O No

If your answer is Yes or Sometimes, it will give you a foreign accent.

Test 68- Say "rest" several times: are your lips fully rounded when you say the letter **r** in "**r**est"?

O Yes O Sometimes O No

If your answer is Yes or Sometimes, you will need to make sure you are not saying "west" when you mean "rest".

Test 69- Say "right" several times: does your pronunciation of "**r**ight" sound like "**l**ight"?

O Yes O Sometimes O No

If your answer is Yes or Sometimes, please note that the meaning of the word changes if you say /l/ instead of /r/.

Test 70- Say "march" several times: do you pronounce the letter **r** in "ma**r**ch"?

O Yes O Sometimes O No

It is okay if your answer is Yes or Sometimes. However, please note that most English people DO NOT say /r/ in words such as "march".

Learn how to make this English sound

Your tongue needs to float in the middle of your mouth while you say the letter **r** in "**r**ed".

There are two ways you can get your tongue floating in the middle of your mouth:

- Curl the tip of your tongue towards the top of your mouth, being careful not to touch or get too close to the top of your mouth

or

- Pull your tongue backwards, being careful not to touch or get too close to the back of your mouth.

Once your tongue is floating in the middle of your mouth, make a sound with your throat.

You will need to round your lips at the start of a word, as in "**r**ed". If you find it difficult to make this sound at the start of a word, follow these steps:

1. Softly bite your lower lip by placing your upper teeth between your lower lip and lower teeth.

red

2. Push your lips out a little.
3. With your mouth in this position, start saying "**r**ed".

The symbol for this sound is /r/. Practise saying "**r**ed, **r**est, **r**ight". You will also need to make this sound when you say the letters **rh**, **wr**, **rr** in "**rh**yme, **wr**ite, co**rr**ect".

What happens with the letter r in "bird, sport, march"?

Most English people ONLY say /r/ when the next sound is a vowel sound. As a result, they NEVER say /r/ in words such as "bird, sport, march".

Does this mean that "sport" sounds like "spot"? The answer is NO because the vowel sound is different.

What happens with the letter r in "car"?

As mentioned before, most English people ONLY say /r/ when the next sound is a vowel sound. As a result, they would NOT say /r/ in "I left my car next to the yellow car". However, they would say /r/ in "His ca**r** is black" because there is a vowel afterwards: "car is".

Interesting note: These native speakers don't think about the appearance or disappearance of the /r/ sound. It happens automatically. Since it happens automatically, some speakers may say /r/ where there should NOT be one as in "I saw a boy" (I saw r a boy).

Watch and repeat

Go to www.HowNotToSay.com/book to watch a video that will help you with this sound.

14

web

web

Identify what gives you a foreign accent

Here are speech habits that you should avoid. You may have several, one, or none of these unwanted habits. Do all the tests to find out!

Test 71- Say "wood" several times: do you pronounce the letter **w** in "**w**ood" with the /g/ sound?

O Yes O Sometimes O No

*If your answer is Yes or Sometimes, your pronunciation of "**w**ood" could be heard as "**g**ood".*

Test 72- Say "west" several times: do your upper teeth touch your lower lip when you say the letter **w** in "**w**est"?

O Yes O Sometimes O No

*If your answer is Yes or Sometimes, your pronunciation of "**w**est" could be heard as "**v**est".*

Test 73- Say "web": do your lips stay still (do not move) while you say the letter **w** in "**w**eb"?

O Yes O Sometimes O No

If your answer is Yes or Sometimes, you need to work on this sound.

Learn how to make this English sound

To learn how to say the letter **w** in "**w**eb" follow these steps:

1. Round your lips as much as possible.
2. With your lips extremely rounded, start making a sound similar to the letters **oo** in "m**oo**n".
3. While making this sound, move your lips from the extremely rounded position to the position needed for the next vowel (**w**e̲b). The movement of your lips is essential to make this sound!

Practise making this sound in "**w**eb, **w**est, **w**atch, **w**ood, **w**olf". The symbol for this sound is /w/. You will also need to make this sound when you say the letters **wh** in "**wh**en, **wh**ite, **wh**at" and the letter **u** in "q**u**ick, q**u**een, freq**u**ent, lang**u**age". The number "one" is also pronounced with a /w/ sound.

If you find it difficult to make the /w/ sound in "**w**ood" and "**w**olf", remember to round your lips as much as possible before saying these words.

Watch and repeat

Go to www.HowNotToSay.com/book to watch a video that will help you with this sound.

15

yes

yes

Identify what gives you a foreign accent

Here are two speech habits that you should avoid.

Test 74- Say "yes" several times: do you press your tongue firmly against the top of your mouth at the beginning of the word "**y**es"?

O Yes O Sometimes O No

*If your answer is Yes or Sometimes, your pronunciation of "**y**es" will give you a foreign accent. And if you press it very hard, your pronunciation of "**y**es" could be heard as "**J**ess".*

Test 75- Say "yes" again: does your tongue stay still (not move) while you say the letter **y** in "**y**es"?

O Yes O Sometimes O No

If your answer is Yes or Sometimes, you need to work on this sound.

Learn how to make this English sound

To learn how to say the letter **y** in "**y**es" follow these steps:

1. Put your upper teeth very close to your lower teeth.
2. Leave the tip of your tongue behind your lower teeth and

put the front of your tongue very close to the top of your mouth.

3. Start making a sound similar to the sound of the letters **ea** in "**ea**t".
4. As soon as you start making this sound, and while you are making this sound, move your tongue and your jaw down towards the position needed for the following sound (**y**e̲s). This movement is essential to make this sound!

Practise making this sound in "**y**es, **y**ou, **y**ear". The symbol for this sound is /j/.

Sometimes you will need to make the /j/ sound before a /u:/ sound (see chapter 20) as in "**u**se, f**ew**, val**ue**, q**ueue**".

Watch and repeat

Go to www.HowNotToSay.com/book to watch a video that will help you with this sound.

16

hello

hello

Identify what gives you a foreign accent

Here are speech habits that you should avoid. You may have several, one, or none of these unwanted habits. Do all the tests to find out!

Test 76- Say "hello" several times: do you make a sound that is harsh (unpleasant to the ear) when you say the letter **h** in "**h**ello"?

O Yes O Sometimes O No

If your answer is Yes or Sometimes, it will give you a strong foreign accent.

Test 77- Say "hot" several times: do you press the back of your tongue firmly against the top of your mouth when you say "**h**ot"?

O Yes O Sometimes O No

If your answer is Yes or Sometimes, it will give you a strong accent.

Test 78- Say "heat" several times: do you say "eat" instead of "**h**eat"?

O Yes O Sometimes O No

If your answer is Yes or Sometimes, you should avoid this although some native speakers do this.

Test 79- Say "hello, hot" several times: is your mouth in the same position when you say the letter **h** in these two words?

O Yes **O** Sometimes **O** No

If your answer is Yes or Sometimes, you need to work on the /h/ sound.

Learn how to make this English sound

Did you know that your mouth needs to be in a different position when you say the letter **h** in "**h**ello" than when you say the letter **h** in "**h**ot"?

The position of your mouth depends on the vowel sound (hello, hot). Follow these steps to say the letter **h** in "**h**ello, **h**ot":

1. Put your mouth in position for the following vowel sound (hello, hot).
2. Before saying the vowel sound, blow air out of your mouth (**h**ello, **h**ot).

Practise saying "**h**ello, **h**ot, **h**eat, be**h**ind, be**h**aviour, alco**h**ol". The symbol for this sound is /h/. You will also need to make this sound when you say the letters **wh** in "**wh**o, **wh**olly, **wh**ole".

Watch and repeat

Go to www.HowNotToSay.com/book to watch a video that will help you with this sound.

17

about

about

Identify what gives you a foreign accent

Here are speech habits that you should avoid. You may have several, one, or none of these unwanted habits. Do all the tests to find out!

Test 80- Say "about, oppose" several times: do you pronounce the letter **o** in "**o**ppose" with a different sound than the letter **a** in "**a**bout"?

O Yes O Sometimes O No

If your answer is Yes or Sometimes, it will NOT ONLY give you a foreign accent, but it will ALSO interfere with the rhythm of English.

Test 81- Say "for" several times: do you always pronounce "for" with a full vowel sound?

O Yes O No

If your answer is Yes, it will NOT ONLY give you a foreign accent, but it will ALSO interfere with the rhythm of English.

Test 82- Say "away" several times: do you say "way"?

O Yes O Sometimes O No

*If your answer is Yes or Sometimes, your pronunciation of "**a**way" will not be clear.*

Learn how to make this English sound

Let's look at the most important sound in English: the **unstressed vowel sound** in "**a**bout". To make this sound follow these steps:

1. Relax your mouth completely. Your mouth will be relaxed while your upper teeth and lower teeth are slightly apart.
2. Make a short and relaxed sound with your throat.

The symbol for this *short and relaxed sound* is /ə/. You will need to make this sound when you say the **unstressed vowel** in many words. Practise making this sound:

- at the beginning of "**a**bout, **o**ppose, **a**way, **o**ffend",
- in the middle of "t**o**day, circ**u**s, mom**e**nt, triumph**a**nt",
- at the end of "sof**a**, pizz**a**, Chin**a**".

This sound is so frequent that sometimes you will need to make it several times in the same word as in "**a**partm**e**nt".

You should also make this sound when you say "**are**, f**or**" in "They **are** looking f**or** John". This is NOT laziness! **This is the way native speakers speak**, and **it is essential to get the rhythm of English right**. If you pronounce these words with a full vowel sound, it will give the impression that you want to draw attention to these words. Here are more words that you will often hear with this sound: "**a**, **a**m, **a**n, **a**nd, **a**s, **a**t, b**u**t, c**a**n, c**ou**ld, d**o**, d**oe**s, fr**o**m, h**er**, **o**f, sh**ou**ld, th**a**n, th**a**t, th**e**, th**e**m, t**o**, **u**s, w**a**s, w**ere**, w**ou**ld, y**our**".

What happens with "teacher, sugar, doctor"?

As crazy as it sounds "teach**er**, sug**ar**, doct**or**" rhyme with "sof**a**". Let's see how this is possible. Most English people don't normally say /r/ in "teach**er**, sug**ar**, doct**or**" (see chapter 13). Therefore, they normally say "teach**e**, sug**a**, doct**o**". The unstressed vowel in these words is pronounced with the same *short and relaxed sound* as the unstressed vowel in "sof**a**". As a result, "teach**e**, sug**a**, doct**o**" rhyme with "sof**a**".

You may hear some English people say the final sound in "teach**e**, sug**a**, doct**o**, sof**a**" with a sound a little longer and keeping the mouth a little more open. However, I have been advised to keep this sound *short and relaxed* at all times.

Watch and repeat

Go to www.HowNotToSay.com/book to watch a video that will help you with this sound.

18

bird

bird

Identify what gives you a foreign accent

Here are speech habits that you should avoid. You may have several, one, or none of these habits. Do all the tests to find out!

Test 83- Say "bird" several times: do you make the /r/ sound when you say "bi**r**d?

O Yes O Sometimes O No

It is okay if your answer is Yes or Sometimes. However, please note that most English people DO NOT say /r/ in "bird".

Test 84- Say "bird" again: do you make a short sound when you say the vowel sound in "b**ir**d"?

O Yes O Sometimes O No

If your answer is Yes or Sometimes, you should avoid this.

Test 85- Say "bird, turn, work" several times: do you pronounce these words with different vowel sounds?

O Yes O Sometimes O No

If your answer is Yes or Sometimes, you need to be careful with the spelling. These words are all pronounced with the same vowel sound.

Learn how to make this English sound

Most English people NEVER say /r/ in "bird" (see chapter 13). The sound you hear when they say the letters **ir** in "b**ir**d" is the sound of the vowel. To learn how to make this vowel sound follow these steps:

1. Relax your mouth. Your mouth will be relaxed while your upper teeth and lower teeth are slightly apart.
2. Make a *long and stressed sound* with your throat.

Practise making this sound when you say the letters **ir** in "b**ir**d, sh**ir**t, g**ir**l". The symbol for this sound is /ɜ:/. You will also need to make this sound when you say the letters **er**, **ur**, **ear**, **or** in "s**er**ve, t**ur**n, l**ear**n, w**or**k".

Watch and repeat

Go to www.HowNotToSay.com/book to watch a video that will help you with this sound.

19

it - **ea**t

it - eat

Identify what gives you a foreign accent

Here are two speech habits that you should avoid.

Test 86- Say "it - eat" and "ship - sheep": does your pronunciation of "**i**t" sound like "**ea**t" or vice-versa? And/or does your pronunciation of "sh**i**p" sound like "sh**ee**p" or vice-versa?

O Yes O Sometimes O No

If your answer is Yes or Sometimes, you need to work on these sounds.

Test 87- Say "tea" several times: do you make a short sound when you say the vowel sound in "t**ea**"?

O Yes O Sometimes O No

If your answer is Yes or Sometimes, you should avoid this.

Learn how to make these English sounds

To learn how to say the letter **i** in "**i**t" follow these steps:

1. Relax your mouth.
2. Smile **a little** so that the corners of your mouth are a little apart.

3. Put the front of your tongue **a little** bit close to the top of your mouth. You can leave the tip of your tongue behind your lower teeth!
4. Make a ***short sound*** with your throat.

Practise making this sound when you say the letter **i** in "**i**t, sh**i**p, ch**i**p". The symbol for this sound is /ɪ/. You will also need to make this sound when you say the letter **y** in "g**y**m", the letter **e** in "**E**ngland" and the letters **ui** in "b**ui**ld".

Did you know that you also need to make this sound when you say the unstressed vowel in "mus**i**c, Al**e**x, carp**e**t, watch**e**s, list**e**d, lett**u**ce, man**a**ge"? Yes, the letter **e** in "Al**e**x, carp**e**t, watch**e**s, list**e**d", the letter **u** in "lett**u**ce" and the letter **a** in "man**a**ge" are all pronounced with this sound.

*

To learn how to say the letters **ea** in "**ea**t" follow these steps:

1. Put your upper and lower teeth together (or almost touching).
2. Smile **a lot** so that the corners of your mouth are far from each other.
3. Put the front of your tongue **very** close to the top of your mouth. You can leave the tip of your tongue behind your lower teeth!
4. Make a ***long sound*** with your throat.

Practise making this sound when you say the letters **ea** in "**ea**t, p**ea**, pl**ea**se". The symbol for this sound is /iː/. You will also need to make this sound when you say the letters **ee**, **ei**, **ie**, **e**, **i** in "b**ee**, perc**ei**ve, th**ie**ve, th**e**se, sard**i**ne".

You may find it especially difficult to make this sound in words such as "sh**ee**p" and "ch**ea**p", as your lips need to be rounded for the letters **sh** in "**sh**eep" and the letters **ch** in "**ch**eap". Follow these steps to help you say the letters **shee** in "**shee**p" and the letters **chea** in "**chea**p":

1. Put your upper and lower teeth together (or almost touching)
2. Round your lips to say the letters **sh** in "**sh**eep" and the letters **ch** in "**ch**eap".
3. With your teeth still together and your lips still rounded, put the corners of your mouth far from each other to make the /iː/ sound (sh**ee**p, ch**ea**p). It will not look like a smile because your lips are rounded!

Are you ready to say "it - eat"?

Practise saying "**i**t - **ea**t", "b**i**n - b**ea**n", "s**i**t - s**ea**t", "sh**i**p - sh**ee**p", "ch**i**p - ch**ea**p".

Hap-pea Birthday!

When I was in my early twenties, I used to complain that the letter **y** in "happ**y**" sounds like the letters **ea** in "p**ea**" but shorter. It turned out to be true in most accents of English! Let's see why.

As we saw earlier, the unstressed vowel in "mus**i**c, Al**e**x, carp**e**t, watch**e**s, list**e**d, lett**u**ce, man**a**ge" is pronounced with the short and relaxed /ɪ/ sound. In theory, the same thing happens with the unstressed vowel in "happ**y**". However, most English people change this sound at the end of a word, as in "happ**y**": they make a sound similar to /iː/, as in "p**ea**", but shorter.

Practise making this sound in "happ**y**, coff**ee**, mon**ey**". You will also hear this sound when "h**e**" and "sh**e**" are not stressed. You may also hear this sound in words like "r**e**act".

Watch and repeat

Go to www.HowNotToSay.com/book to watch a video that will help you with these sounds.

20

good - food

g**oo**d - f**oo**d

Identify what gives you a foreign accent

Here are two speech habits that you should avoid.

Test 88- Say "good - food" several times: do you pronounce the letters **oo** in "g**oo**d" the same way as in "f**oo**d"?

O Yes **O** Sometimes **O** No

*If your answer is Yes or Sometimes, you need to be careful with the spelling. The vowel sound is different in "g**oo**d" and "f**oo**d".*

Test 89- Say "blue" several times: do you make a short sound when you say the vowel sound in "bl**ue**"?

O Yes **O** Sometimes **O** No

If your answer is Yes or Sometimes, you need to work on this sound.

Learn how to make these English sounds

To learn how to say the letters **oo** in "g**oo**d" follow these steps:

1. Relax your mouth.
2. Round your lips a little.
3. Put the back of your tongue up a little.
4. Make a *short sound* with your throat.

Practise making this sound when you say the letters **oo** in "g**oo**d, l**oo**k, b**oo**k, c**oo**k, t**oo**k, f**oo**t". The symbol for this sound is /ʊ/. You will also need to make this sound when you say the letter **u** in "f**u**ll, p**u**t, p**u**sh" and the letter **o** in "w**o**lf".

*

To learn how to say the letters **oo** in "f**oo**d" follow these steps:

1. Round your lips a lot.
2. Bring your lips together forming a very small circle.
3. Make a *long sound* with your throat.

Practise making this sound when you say the letters **oo** in "f**oo**d, r**oo**m, sch**oo**l, f**oo**l, sm**oo**th, t**oo**th". The symbol for this sound is /u:/. You will also need to make this sound when you say the letters **ew**, **ough**, **wo**, **oe**, **ue**, **ui**, **ou** in "cr**ew**, thr**ough**, t**wo**, sh**oe**, bl**ue**, fr**ui**t, gr**ou**p" and the letters **o**, **u** in "pr**o**ve, L**u**ke".

Sometimes you will need to make the /j/ sound (see chapter 15) before the /u:/ sound as in "**u**se, f**ew**, val**ue**, q**ueue**".

Are you ready to say "good - food"?

Practise saying "g**oo**d - f**oo**d", "l**oo**k - L**u**ke", "f**u**ll - f**oo**l".

Watch and repeat

Go to www.HowNotToSay.com/book to watch a video that will help you with these sounds.

21

spot - sport

sp**o**t - sp**o**rt

Identify what gives you a foreign accent

Here are two speech habits that you should avoid.

Test 90- Say "spot - sport" several times: do you pronounce the letter **o** in "sp**o**t" the same way as in "sp**o**rt"?

O Yes O Sometimes O No

If your answer is Yes or Sometimes, you need to work on these sounds.

Test 91- Say "door" several times: do you make a short sound when you say the letters **oo** in "d**oo**r"?

O Yes O Sometimes O No

If your answer is Yes or Sometimes, you need to change this.

Learn how to make these English sounds

To learn how to say the letter **o** in "sp**o**t" follow these steps:

1. Open your mouth.
2. Round your lips a little.
3. Pull your tongue backwards and downwards.
4. Make a *short sound* with your throat.

Practise making this sound when you say the letter **o** in "sp**o**t, h**o**td**o**g, b**o**x, wr**o**ng, g**o**t, r**o**ck". The symbol for this sound is /ɒ/. You will also need to make this sound when you say the letter **a** in "w**a**sh".

*

Let's look at the word "sport". Most English people NEVER say /r/ in "sport" (see chapter 13). The sound you hear when they say the letters **or** in "sp**or**t" is the sound of the vowel. To learn how to make this vowel sound follow these steps:

1. Round your lips a lot.
2. Bring your lips together forming a small circle.
3. Pull your tongue backwards.
4. Make a *long sound* with your throat.

Practise making this sound when you say the letters **or** in "sp**or**t, sh**or**t, c**or**d". The symbol for this sound is /ɔː/.

You will also need to make this sound when you say the letters **oor**, **our**, **ore**, **ar** in "d**oor**, f**our**, m**ore**, w**ar**". You will ONLY need to say /r/ in "door, four, more, war" when the next word starts with a vowel sound as in "door opens", "four eggs", "more apples", "war and peace".

The letter **a** in "t**a**ll, **a**lready, **a**lways", the letters **al** in "w**al**k, t**al**k, st**al**k" and the letters **aw**, **au**, **oa**, **ou** in "l**aw**, P**au**l, br**oa**d, br**ou**ght" are also pronounced with the /ɔː/ sound.

Are you ready to say "spot - sport"?

Practise saying "sp**o**t - sp**or**t", "sh**o**t - sh**or**t", "c**o**d - "c**or**d".

Watch and repeat

Go to www.HowNotToSay.com/book to watch a video that will help you with these sounds.

22

m**u**ch - m**a**tch - m**ar**ch

m**u**ch - m**a**tch - m**ar**ch

Identify what gives you a foreign accent

Here are speech habits that you should avoid. You may have several, one, or none of these habits. Do all the tests to find out!

Test 92- Say "much, match" several times: does your pronunciation of "m**u**ch" sound like "m**a**tch" or vice-versa?

O Yes O Sometimes O No

*If your answer is Yes or Sometimes, you need to work on the vowel sound in "m**u**ch" and/or the vowel sound in "m**a**tch".*

Test 93- Say "march, match, much" several times: do you pronounce the letter **a** in "m**ar**ch" the same way as the letter **a** in "m**a**tch" or the letter **u** in "m**u**ch"?

O Yes O Sometimes O No

*If your answer is Yes or Sometimes, you need to work on the vowel sound in "m**ar**ch".*

Test 94- Say "car" several times: do you make a short sound when you say the letter **a** in "c**ar**"?

O Yes O Sometimes O No

If your answer is Yes or Sometimes, you need to change this.

Test 95- Say "bad" several times: does your pronunciation of "b**a**d" sound like "b**e**d"?

O Yes **O** Sometimes **O** No

If your answer is Yes or Sometimes, you might need to work on this sound.

Learn how to make these English sounds

Let's look at how to say the letter **u** in "m**u**ch", the letter **a** in "m**a**tch" and the letters **ar** in "m**ar**ch".

*

The sound of the letter **u** in "m**u**ch" varies greatly among speakers of English.

Don't be surprised if you hear native speakers saying the letter **u** in "m**u**ch" with a sound similar to the vowel in "g**oo**d".

For some native speakers, the sound of the letter **u** in "m**u**ch" is similar to the sound of the letter **a** in "**a**bout".

For other native speakers, the sound of the letter **u** in "m**u**ch" is more open. To make this sound follow these steps:

1. Open your mouth.
2. Relax your lips.
3. Leave the tip of your tongue behind your lower teeth.
4. Make a a *short sound* with your throat.

Practise saying the letter **u** in "m**u**ch, **u**p, **u**mbrella". The symbol for this sound is /ʌ/. You will also need to make this sound when you say the letters **ou** in "y**ou**ng, en**ou**gh, t**ou**ch", the letter **o** in "s**o**me, d**o**ne, l**o**ve" and "m**o**ney, **o**nion, L**o**ndon", the letters **oe** in "d**oe**s" and the letters **oo** in "fl**oo**d".

*

To learn how to say the letter **a** in "m**a**tch" follow these steps:

1. Open your mouth.
2. Pull the corners of your mouth away from each other. Make sure they are far apart.
3. Put your tongue at the bottom of your mouth, with the tip of your tongue behind your lower teeth.
4. Make a *short sound* with your throat.

Practise making this sound when you say the letter **a** in "m**a**tch, **a**pple, **a**nimal, **a**llergy". The symbol for this sound is /æ/. You will also need to make this sound when you say the letters **al** in "s**al**mon".

This sound is classified as a *short sound*. However, some English people make it quite long in words such like "d**a**d, b**a**g, b**a**d".

*

Let's look at the word "march". Most English people NEVER say /r/ in "march" (see chapter 13). The sound you hear when they say the letters **ar** in "m**ar**ch" is the sound of the vowel. To learn how to make this vowel sound follow these steps:

1. Open your mouth.
2. Pull your tongue backwards and downwards.
3. Make a *long sound* with your throat.

The symbol for this sound is /ɑː/. Practise making this sound when you say the letters **ar** in "m**ar**ch, g**ar**den, **ar**m", the letters **ear** in "h**ear**t" and the letters **er** in "s**er**geant".

You will also need to make this sound when you say the letters **ar** in "c**ar**, st**ar**, f**ar**". You will ONLY need to say /r/ in "car, star, far" when the next word starts with a vowel sound as in "car insurance", "star of the show", "far away".

The letters **al** in "p**al**m, c**al**m, b**al**m" and the letter **a** in "f**a**ther" are also pronounced with the /ɑ:/ sound.

Many English people also say /ɑ:/ in "l**au**gh, b**a**th, **a**fter, **a**sk, h**al**f". However, some native speakers pronounce "laugh, bath, after, ask, half" with the same vowel sound as in "match".

Are you ready to say "much - match - march"?

Practise saying:

- "m**u**ch - m**a**tch - m**ar**ch"
- "c**u**t - c**a**t - c**ar**t"

Watch and repeat

Go to www.HowNotToSay.com/book to watch a video that will help you with these sounds.

23

pen

pen

Identify what gives you a foreign accent

Here is one speech habit you may need to avoid.

Test 96- Say "pen" several times: is your mouth relaxed when you say the letter **e** in "p**e**n"?

O Yes O Sometimes O No

If your answer is Yes or Sometimes, you need to work on this vowel sound.

Learn how to make this English sound

To learn how to say the letter **e** in "p**e**n" follow these steps:

1. Open your mouth.
2. Smile so that the corners of your mouth are far from each other.
3. You can leave the tip of your tongue behind your lower teeth.
4. Make a *short sound* with your throat.

Practise making this sound in "p**e**n, **e**gg, b**e**d". The symbol for this sound is /e/. You will also need to make this sound when you say the letters **ea** in "h**ea**d, r**ea**dy, w**ea**ther", the letter **a** in "m**a**ny, River Th**a**mes", the letters **ie** in "fr**ie**nd" and the letters **ai** in "s**ai**d". Most native speakers also make this sound when they say the letters **ay** in "s**ay**s".

Watch and repeat

Go to www.HowNotToSay.com/book to watch a video that will help you with this sound.

24

no - n**ow** - sk**y** -
b**oy** - Sp**ai**n -
n**ear** - p**air** - t**our**

no - now - sky - boy - Spain - near - pair - tour

Identify what gives you a foreign accent

Here are speech habits that you should avoid. You may have several, one, or none of these unwanted habits. Do all the tests to find out!

Test 97- Say "no" several times: do you pronounce the letter **o** in "n**o**" with a single sound?

O Yes O Sometimes O No

If your answer is Yes or Sometimes, you need to change this.

Test 98- Say "no, now, sky, boy, Spain, near, pair, tour" with *double vowel sounds*: do you make the second part of English *double vowel sounds* as long as, or longer than, the first part?

O Yes O Sometimes O No

If your answer is Yes or Sometimes, you will need to work on these English double vowel sounds.

Test 99- Look at yourself in the mirror and say "now, Spain": are your lips relaxed when you start making the *double vowel sound* in "n**ow**, Sp**ai**n"?

O Yes O Sometimes O No

If your answer is Yes or Sometimes, you need to change this.

Learn how to make these English sounds

Let's look at the English *double vowel sounds.*

*

English people pronounce the letter **o** in "n**o**" with a *double vowel sound*. To make this *double sound* follow these steps:

1. Start making a sound with your mouth relaxed. Your mouth will be relaxed while your upper teeth and lower teeth are slightly apart.
2. Keep making this sound. In English, the first part of a *double vowel sound* is longer than its second part.
3. Smoothly round your lips a little. This second part of the *double sound* is similar to the vowel sound in "g**oo**d".

Practise making this *double sound* when you say the letter **o** in "n**o**, g**o**, s**o**" and "**o**kay, m**o**st, hell**o**". The symbol for this sound is /əʊ/. You will also need to make this *double sound* when you say the letters **ow**, **oa**, **ou**, **ough**, **oe**, **o** in "sn**ow**, r**oa**d, m**ou**ld, alth**ough**, t**oe**, ph**o**ne".

*

English people pronounce the letters **ow** in "n**ow**" with a *double vowel sound*. To make this *double sound* follow these steps:

1. Start with a sound similar to the vowel in "m**a**tch", opening your mouth a lot and placing the corners of your mouth far from each other.
2. Keep making this sound. In English, the first part of a *double vowel sound* is longer than its second part.
3. Smoothly round your lips a little while closing your mouth a little. This second part of the *double sound* is similar to the vowel sound in "g**oo**d".

Practise making this *double sound* when you say the letters **ow** in "n**ow**, t**ow**n, c**ow**". The symbol for this sound is /aʊ/.

You will also need to make this *double sound* when you say the letters **ou** in "**ou**t, h**ou**se". This is also the sound English people make when they get hurt!

*

English people pronounce the letter **y** in "sk**y**" with a *double vowel sound*. To make this *double sound* follow these steps:

1. Start making this sound with your mouth open but your lips relaxed.
2. Keep making this sound. In English, the first part of a *double vowel sound* is longer than its second part.
3. Smoothly pull the corners of your mouth a little bit apart. This second part of the *double sound* is similar to the vowel sound in "**i**t".

Practise making this *double sound* when you say "sk**y**, tr**y**, wh**y**". You will also need to make this sound when you say the letter **i** in "f**i**nd, f**i**ve" and the letters **ie**, **uy** in "p**ie**, b**uy**".

The symbol for this sound is /aɪ/. Although this symbol is similar to /aʊ/, your lips should be relaxed at the start of /aɪ/.

*

English people pronounce the letters **oy** in "b**oy**" with a *double vowel sound*. To make this *double sound* follow these steps:

1. Make a sound similar to the vowel in "sp**or**t", with your lips rounded forming a small circle (but not as small a circle as in "sp**or**t").
2. Keep making this sound. In English, the first part of a *double vowel sound* is longer than its second part.
3. Smoothly pull the corners of your mouth a little bit apart. This second part of the *double sound* is similar to the vowel in "**i**t".

Practise making this *double sound* when you say the letters **oy** in "b**oy**, t**oy**, **oy**ster". The symbol for this sound is /ɔɪ/. You will also need to make this sound when you say the letters **oi** in "p**oi**nt, c**oi**n, j**oi**n".

*

English people pronounce the letters **ai** in "Sp**ai**n" with a *double vowel sound*. To make this *double sound* follow these steps:

1. Start with a sound similar to the vowel in "b**e**d", with your mouth open and a smile.
2. Keep making this sound. In English, the first part of a *double vowel sound* is longer than its second part.
3. Smoothly pull the corners of your mouth just a little bit apart. This second part of the *double sound* is similar to the vowel in "**i**t".

Practise making this *double sound* when you say "Sp**ai**n, r**ai**n, w**ai**t". The symbol for this sound is /eɪ/. You will also need to make this sound when you say the letter **a** in "**a**ngel, n**a**me" and the letters **eigh**, **ey**, **ea**, **ay** in "**eigh**t, th**ey**, gr**ea**t, d**ay**".

*

Most English people don't normally say /r/ in "near" (see chapter 13). The sound they normally make for the letters **ear** in "n**ear**" is a *double vowel sound*. To make this *double sound*:

1. Start with a sound similar to the vowel in "**i**t" or in "**ea**t", with the corners of your mouth a little bit apart.
2. Keep making this sound. In English, the first part of a *double vowel sound* is longer than its second part.
3. Smoothly relax your mouth.

Practise making this *double sound* when you say the letters **ear** in "n**ear**, h**ear**, **ear**". The symbol for this sound is /ɪə/.

*

Most English people don't normally say /r/ in "pair" (see chapter 13). The sound they normally make for the letters **air** in "p**air**" is a *double vowel sound*. To make this *double sound* follow these steps:

1. Start with a sound similar to the vowel in "b**e**d", with your mouth open and a smile.
2. Keep making this sound. In English, the first part of a *double vowel sound* is longer than its second part.
3. Smoothly relax your mouth.

Practise making this *double sound* when you say the letters **air** in "p**air**, h**air**, **air**". Do the same for the letters **are**, **ear**, **ere** in "c**are**, b**ear**, th**ere**". The symbol for this sound is /eə/.

Nowadays, some English people replace this *double sound* with one long /e/ sound.

*

Most English people don't normally say /r/ in "tour" (see chapter 13). The sound they normally make for the letters **our** in "t**our**" is a *double vowel sound*. To make this *double sound*:

1. Start with a sound similar to the vowel in "g**oo**d", rounding your lips a little.
2. Keep making this sound. In English, the first part of a *double vowel sound* is longer than its second part.
3. Smoothly relax your mouth.

Practise making this *double sound* when you say the letters **our**, **ure**, **oor** in "t**our**, s**ure**, p**oor**". The symbol for this sound is /ʊə/.

Nowadays, many English people replace this *double sound* with the *long sound* found in "sp**or**t".

Watch and repeat

Go to www.HowNotToSay.com/book to watch a video that will help you with these sounds.

25

i**s**land

i**s**land

Identify what gives you a foreign accent

Here is one more habit that you should avoid.

Test 100- Say "island, talk, psychology": do you pronounce the letter **s** in "i**s**land", the letter **l** in "ta**l**k" and/or the letter **p** in "**p**sychology"?

O Yes **O** Sometimes **O** No

If your answer is Yes or Sometimes, you will need to be careful with the spelling.

What happens with the letter s in "island"?

The letter **s** in "i**s**land" is silent, that is, you DO NOT have to say anything for the letter **s** in "i**s**land". The same thing happens with the following letters:

- the letter **l** in "ta**l**k"
- the letter **p** in "**p**sychology"
- the letter **b** in "dou**b**t"
- the letter **t** in "lis**t**en"
- the letter **k** in "**k**now"
- the letter **c** in "s**c**ene"

- the letter **g** in "sign"
- the letter **n** in "autumn"
- the letter **w** in "Greenwich"
- the letter **h** in "hour"
- The letter **e** in "five"

It is important to note that the letter **e** is always silent at the end of an English word. If you see the letter **e** at the end of a word, the chances are that the word needs to be pronounced with a *long vowel sound* as in "l*ea*v**e**, L*u*k**e**" or a *double vowel sound* as in "ph*o*n**e**, h*ou*s**e**, f*i*v**e**, n*a*m**e**". Having said that, the letter **e** also appears at the end of words such as "l*o*v**e**, s*o*m**e**, d*o*n**e**".

Watch and repeat

Go to www.HowNotToSay.com/book to watch a video that will help you with these words.

Symbols

English spelling is very misleading. Many dictionaries use symbols to show you what sounds to make in each word. Here is a summary of the symbols and keywords used in this book.

Chapter 1:	/f/ **f**an	/v/ **v**an
Chapter 2:	/θ/ **th**anks	/ð/ **th**ey
Chapter 3:	/s/ **s**ip	/z/ **z**ip
Chapter 4:	/ʃ/ **sh**ip	/ʒ/ televi**si**on
Chapter 5:	/p/ **p**ea	/b/ **b**ee
Chapter 6:	/k/ **c**old	/g/ **g**old
Chapter 7:	/t/ **t**own	/d/ **d**own
Chapter 8:	/tʃ/ **ch**ain	/dʒ/ **J**ane
Chapter 9:	/m/ albu**m**	
Chapter 10:	/n/ **n**et	
Chapter 11:	/ŋ/ si**ng**	
Chapter 12:	/l/ **l**ast	

Chapter 13:	/r/ **r**ed		
Chapter 14:	/w/ **w**eb		
Chapter 15:	/j/ **y**es		
Chapter 16:	/h/ **h**ello		
Chapter 17:	/ə/ **a**bout		
Chapter 18:	/ɜː/ b**ir**d		
Chapter 19:	/ɪ/ **i**t	/iː/ **ea**t	
Chapter 20:	/ʊ/ g**oo**d	/uː/ f**oo**d	
Chapter 21:	/ɒ/ sp**o**t	/ɔː/ sp**or**t	
Chapter 22:	/ʌ/ m**u**ch	/æ/ m**a**tch	/ɑː/ m**ar**ch
Chapter 23:	/e/ p**e**n		
Chapter 24:	/əʊ/ n**o**	/aʊ/ n**ow**	/aɪ/ sk**y**
	/ɔɪ/ b**oy**	/eɪ/ Sp**ai**n	/ɪə/n**ear**
	/eə/ p**air**	/ʊə/ t**our**	

What next?

Congratulations! You have reached the end of this book. What do you need to do now?

Practise, practise, practise

Keep practising the sounds covered in this book until you can make them automatically.

You will find more material to help you practise at **www.HowNotToSay.com/book**.

Acknowledgements

This book could not have come into being without the help and support of many people. I would like to express my gratitude to:

- David Bauckham, a native voice teacher from London, for happily helping me with my endless list of questions and checking the final copy of this book
- Lucie McGowan-Docherty, an English teacher and proofreader in Nottingham, for patiently going through the final copy of this book and giving me feedback
- Emma Tootell, a speech therapist in Nottingham, for advising me to speak slowly and for helping me pronounce the last sound in "ba**g**, be**d**, la**b**, bri**dge**"
- the readers of my Spanish blog for giving me the strength to work on this project
- my friends, in particular, Celia, Fabiola, Indu, Lodka, Magaly and Vanesa for reading early copies of this book and providing me with invaluable feedback
- Helen, my mother-in-law, for copy editing this book
- my husband and two children for being so loving, kind and supportive.

Printed in Poland
by Amazon Fulfillment
Poland Sp. z o.o., Wrocław

67469179R00078